The Ohs and Aahs of Aging

Revised Edition
(With more Ohs and less Oops)

Sharon Wolfe
Illustrations by: Saul L. Miller

All rights reserved

No part of this publication may be reproduced or stored in a retrieval system or transmitted by any means without written permission of the author, except by reviewer who may quote brief passages in a review.

Permission requests should be emailed to:
smwolfe@rogers.com

ISBN: 9781798121245
Printing: March 2019, February 2020, February 2022

This book is dedicated
to everyone
who finds life best
when we smile our way through it

A Tribute to Friendship

Ode to friends who've stuck with us
through days of pain and glory.
Ode to their devoted support
that sees us though our story.
In all we share, the fun and falls
that contribute to each life
they've joined us in our laughter
they've wiped our tears of strife.

Ode to those together times
when our babes were young.
Learning to be mothers
to each other we had clung.
Unsure we were of what to do
relieved, we had each other,
to see us through the scary days
as we learned to be a mother.

Ode to friends who accompanied us
through our middle years,
who witnessed changes happening
as we grew and shifted gears.
Ode to knowing they will keep
the secrets of our heart.
Ode to the valued wisdom
with such care they did impart.

Ode to friends at this time now
when lives are almost spent.
Ode to their understanding
when we begin to vent
about the aches and losses.
They listen, and when we moan,
they comfort and ensure us, that
in old age - we aren't alone.

Ode to you devoted angels
who encircle us with love.
Ode to you -- forever friends
our life-lines from above.
To all of you, who've enriched us so,
whose gifts enhance our living,
this poem we dedicate to you.
It is a tribute to your giving.

My Pretty's Upped and Left Me

My pretty's upped and left me,
gone with wind
that blew though time.
Scattering debris upon my face,
here a sunspot--there a line.

My pretty's upped and left me,
with gravity's kisses
it took its leave.
And with it went the compliments
at times I did receive.

My pretty's upped and left me,
Now people are more inclined
to think before they comment
left they appear unkind.

"I can't believe you're eighty.
For eighty you sure look great.
I swear no one would give you
one day past seventy-eight!"

We Can Get Used to Anything

We can get used to anything
Retirement,
loss of prestige, purpose, pay-check.
Dreams which didn't materialize,
problems that did.
Having too much time
and not enough days.

We can get used to anything
Aching backs, stiffening joints,
cortisone shots and wonky hips.
Diets eliminating flavor
in favor
of lowering cholesterol.

We can get used to anything
Being oldest at family reunions.
Children living in the distance.
Empty houses once called homes.
Wisdom earned
that no one cares to hear.

We can get used to anything
Grown children
moving back home.
Petty daughters-in-law
who misinterpret our suggestions.
Ex-s we once loved
who are no longer part of us.

We can get used to anything
Matinees,
no nighttime driving.
Names-remembered or not.
Computer skills
source of grandchild's amusement.

Yes, we can get used to anything
Anything that life throws at us.
We all can ... With one exception.
We can never get used to
reaching out to phone
someone who is no longer here.

I'm Free

I'm older and I love it.
It's better than I did foresee.
I no longer answer to others.
I'm free. Yes, really free.

I love pants with stretchy waists.
I love to wear flat shoes.
I love that I can do…whatever,
whenever, I choose.

So what if I have wrinkles.
So what if I'm kind of fat.
So what if my hair is thinning,
I look pretty in a hat.

That's why you'll never hear me say
words like "woe is me".
I'm too busy enjoying myself.
I'm free. I'm really free!

Ode to the Aging Bladder

Behold the aging bladder
which dribbles forth on cue.
A laugh, a cry, a hiccup
there's little we can do,
to stop the flow,
to hide the shame,
to ignore, or to forget,
to carry on with dignity
as if our pants aren't wet.

Dearly Departed

I've said good-bye to John and Joan,
to Evie and friend Steve.
To Rob and Glady and jolly Mel
All of whom, I grieve.

Ralph and Stan and Ian too,
Shuffled off this mortal coil.
Arlene's death was a surprise
Norm's left us in turmoil.

It's loss of friends I most regret
about these Golden Years.
The inevitable of what we face
speaks to my biggest fears.

For there's no escaping it,
more losses are still in store
for those of us, lucky enough,
to live three score plus more.

Thus, Saith The Lord

If your children do not listen
don't worry, it's just their way.
It's been like this since time began,
as the Good Lord, Himself did say.

"Think of all the wisdom
in my Almighty head
you think I'd be listened to
by my children ...
                but instead,
my first son, my Adam,
shunned my Fatherly advice.
He allowed the temptress Eve
with an apple to entice...
                him away from all I gave,
regardless of consequence."

This goes to show there is no point
in continuing to dispense
advice that won't be heeded...
It's best to save ourselves from woe
and let our darlings fly the coop,
without sharing all we know.

It's Here - Somewhere.

I'll be there in a moment
just need to find my keys,
don't remember where I put them
thanks to my brain freeze.

Here they are, I've got them,
I'll be ready in just a sec,
as soon as I find my sweater
the one with the open neck.

I hung it in the cupboard
or did I put it in the drawer?
I hate when this is happening
it frustrates me to the core.

Some people say, "Just focus,
stop and think of what you do."
I know what they're suggesting
is a valid point of view.

But I'm always in a hurry
doing one thing or another,
so, I rarely pay attention
to those things I'll need recover.

Great, I have my sweater now
I'm ready. We can go.
Wait. Where are my keys?
They were here just moments ago.

Egad, I'm Turning 80

Egad, I'm turning eighty!
Could say "I can't believe"
but as a wannabe poet
surely up my sleeve
exist some gems awaiting
that are not old and stale,
to describe this coming decade.
Something on the scale
of words poets would utter
which would be cited to this day,
that would satisfy my ego,
raise me above the fray.
Then I'd be a for-real poet,
not a verse-y wannabe,
and turning eighty would become
a gift from I to me.

Zuckerberg oh Zuckerberg

Zuckerberg, oh Zuckerberg
that brainy little kid,
unleased a scary monster.
That's really what he did.
Now grandkids only like to chat
with those they know on line,
"Don't take it personally"
they're apt to say,
when together we do dine.
We watch them and we wonder,
can they still converse
face to face
without their gadgets?
Sometimes, I fear the worse.
Determined, I advise myself,
as I so often do,
"Accept that life is different now,
and it's solely up to you...
You can opt to have your say.
But should you hold your tongue,
you'll enhance
your special place
in the hearts of all your young."
So, I bite my tongue and promise,
whenever they choose to come,
I'll refrain from
useless bitching.
I'll savour every crumb.

Staying Relevant

When I retired, left friends behind,
I found myself in quite a bind.
Without my work I was not content
afraid I'd become irrelevant.

To stave off feelings of ennui,
I decided to create a new-old-me.
Knowing boredom would be resolved
only if I were involved...

I searched about for authentic ways
to fill and enrich my empty days.
Soon found friends, to my distress
suffering under much duress.

Some were ill. Some lost their zeal.
Some bore a loneliness I could feel.
And so, my new job began
as go-to person for my fellow man.

Drop-in visits prove good for some
who feel less lonely when I come.
I cook, give lifts, go to the store
or do whatever is called for.

While keeping busy in this way
It's amazing how quickly goes the day.
I no longer yearn for the time that was.
I like where I'm at, and that's because...
giving to others, gives more back to me
enriching my life as I didn't foresee.

Friendly Advice

Not meaning to be condescending
With the hope I'm not offending
In this rhyme that I am sending
to all of you,
I'm recommending...

Because the way things are trending
we oldies need stop pretending
that our lives aren't close to ending.
And if we wish for
years extending...

We must clearly be intending
to save the energy we're expending
on silly things like not befriending
those,
who though not intending...
May have hurt us in some way.

OLD QUESTION – NEW TWIST

A sweet little boy
with the bluest of eyes,
looked up at the granddad
he thought was so wise.
"What will you be?"
Asked the boy with a frown,
"When you get older
and you grow down?"

Names: The First to Go

What a pain in the butt
this old memory of mine.
Try though I do
I must resign
myself, to the fact,
that I've grown so old
my recall is sketchy.
It blows hot and cold.

Does it start with an A?
or is it an L?
I just need a moment
I know it so well.
I hate when this happens
when a name escapes me.
Wait, it's coming...
          I've got it!
"Hi there, Anna-Lee."

Panning for Gold

We've reached a time or so I've been told
that's packed to the brim with nuggets of gold.
The nugget of 'freedom' – like a breath of fresh air
is just one of the treasures that await us there.

There are goodies galore in this new habitat
where we can do what we want, sans set-format.
We can go to bed early. Sleep in if we choose.
Needn't wait until evening to dip into the booze.

We no longer ask of ourselves - perfection.
We fear neither critics or abject rejection.
We eat what we want, though somewhat less.
If kale's not on the menu, we don't distress.

We get senior discounts where ever we go.
No longer tell kids what we think they need know.
We dress for comfort, don't care about size.
When not in the mood, we don't moisturize.

Don't bother with gadgets, use the phone on a wall.
Our greatest joy is when grandkiddies call.
We never complain that our memories are shot,
we're too busy rereading the books we forgot.

When life's aging glitches knock us around
our positive attitudes help us rebound
as we keep on panning for the nuggets of gold
that we've earned and deserved -- now that we're old.

Oops-a-Daisy

"Oops-a-daisy," I used to say
when my toddler had a fall.
I'd pick him up, hug him tight,
and in no time at all
he'd be off and running
returning to his play.
The boo-boo long forgotten
just another normal day.

But oops-a-daisy weren't words I used
when I had my fall.
Words that came to my mind then
quite frankly could appall
anyone who heard them.
But on this they would agree--
FALLING DOWN's too frequent,
when one's passed seventy-three.

My friends said "You were lucky.
You could have been alone.
You could've shattered both your hips,
but only broke a bone."
No truer words were spoken
it always could be worse.
So, next time I'll "oops-a-daisy" me
and supress the urge to curse.

Hopefully

Surprise Encounters

Something weird has happened.
Something strange snuck up on me.
I didn't see it coming
there was no way I could foresee
the future day when kids of mine
grown-up would turn the page
and quietly, without fan-fare
take their place in middle age.

Yet that's exactly what they did.
Without warning, one awesome day
I saw my daughter dripping wet,
with concern I had to say,
"Are you ill? Is that the reason
causing you to sweat?"
My daughter smiling shook her head
"It's menopause, don't fret."

"Menopause!
      She must be kidding.
When did she reach that stage?
I know time passes rapidly --
but my daughter?
      Now middle age?

Then before I could adjust myself
to this new reality,
another surprise was in the wings
all-set to rattle me.

My sons appeared upon the scene,
one balding, the other grey,
both sporting midlife paunches.
How long have they looked this way?
When did my delicious boys
disappear without a trace?
When did these grown-up men
sneak in to take their place?

Eventually, when the shock died down,
I was as pleased as pleased could be,
realizing my children are growing old,
so as to keep in step with me.

A Loss Like No Other - In Three Parts

The Widow

Bereaved, I grieved
For I never conceived
The emptiness of life without you

The Jilted

Bereaved, I grieved
'Till I finally perceived
You weren't worth the effort.

The Aged One

Bereaved, I grieved
I wouldn't have believed
My mirror would turn so cruelly against me.

Planning Ahead

I constantly strive to be healthy,
to eat well and do exercise.
I sleep, I nap, and do whatever else
my team of specialists advise.

Because according to recent statists,
I can live to a hundred and one.
So, I must remain quite healthy
        Lest,
I spoil the old age - of my son.

Down, Down, Down it Goes

The largest organ is our skin
so, it comes as no surprise
when visited by gravity
it will, in time ... capsize.
The face goes first as well you know,
but gravity's never done,
skin keeps falling in its wake
sparing not a one.
It sags on down 'till it does fold
itself, upon one's ankles old.
Those folds appear, as I can attest,
when wearing shoes ...
                    So, may I suggest
that woman of a certain age
before buying shoes,
          stop
              and
                  engage
the mirrors placed on the shoe-shop floor,
they'll tell you true, that's what they're for.

Look straight on, then to the side,
that will help you to decide,
for if some drooping skin you view
you'll know to bid those shoes "adieu."
And search again until you find
a design of a different kind.
Camouflage is what you need,
find that, then confidently proceed
to buy those babies, for you'll know,
you aced the purchase, by going slow.

Ode to My Final Dinner Party

Mary can't eat gluten.
There's Frank who won't eat meats.
Susie gets hives from chicken,
and Al a rash from beets.
Sam Schwartz said he's kosher.
Mohamed eats halal.
Ann's lactose intolerant.
Shanaya requested dahl.
The Steins are both vegans.
And Rhoda's on a diet.
Carol won't eat fish.
And Harvey will not try it…
if it's green or looking healthy
or if it isn't fried.
I asked - and now I'm stymied.
No way can I decide
what to serve for dinner
to this fussy crew.
I'd like to cancel outright,
but that's not the thing to do.
Instead I'll make a buffet
with a bit for everyone.
And then my dinner party days,
will be forever done.

Cosmetic Enhancement

I once had surgery to erase
what age had done to my face.
Then years passed and behold
once again, I looked so old.

So, to the surgeon back I went,
my frustration I did vent.
"Relax," he said, "You I can please,
but it will cost at least ten gees."

"Will it last?" I asked of him.
"The outlook," he said, "is rather slim.
It's life, my dear, get used to it.
In time we all, will look like shit."

How Can it Be?

So said the dentist,
"Your enamel is thinning"

So said the beautician,
"Your nose hair needs trimming"

"You've lost two inches,"
the doctor said.
While hairs keep falling from off
my head.

Which leaves me to wonder
if this is my fate
If I'm losing so much,
Why am I gaining this weight?

Changing Weather

One grey and gloomy morning
she was feeling like the weather.
She missed her husband terribly,
fifty years they'd been together.

On that same dark, dreary day,
the old gent was feeling blue.
Loneliness was consuming him.
He thought his life was through.

They both had promised children
who did worry so,
They'd attend bereavement group,
though neither wished to go.

One bleak day they left their homes
and when they did arrive,
fortune must have intervened
for they were seated side by side.

Each thought the other nice
so, when it was time for tea,
they sought each other out
and spoke, quite tentatively.

Then other meetings followed,
being together soon seemed right.
As their loneliness did vanish,
    once days of grey, grew bright.

Decidedly Done

New Year's Resolutions aren't for me
I think they are a travesty.
Why set myself up to fail
when lacking discipline to nail
the promises to self I make,
which in time I'm bound to break?

I can't diet. Hate the gym.
Give up vodka? The chance is slim!
Sleep eight hours, is not for me
when I often wake to pee.
Sure, I've promised to buy less
saving Visa-bill distress.
Planned to walk on past the store,
seconds later was through their door.

Experience gained, wise I've become
and joyfully now conclude
what works for some will not suit
my particular aptitude.
So, I no longer follow trends
especially when the effect
is bound to shake my confidence
and demean my self-respect.

Myth Busters

Rhoda runs marathons.
Marlene, she crochets.
Carol weaves tallit bags.
Barb's known for her soufflés.

Sheila rides upon her horse.
Joyce chooses to rock-climb.
Sally plays a round of golf.
Sue water-paints full-time.

Ann does meals-on-wheels.
Nan's getting her degree.
Gail is in a zoomba class,
while Denise prefers Tai Chi.

We're busy and we're active.
See our golden glow.
It comes with the freedom
and also 'because we know...

We will not be sitting
in the proverbial rocking chair.
We're far too busy living life
with a golden-oldie flare!

The Visit

She visits him every day
although he knows her naught.
She sits with him and holds his hand
not because she ought
but rather 'cause he was her love
her soulmate of yesteryear
and though his mind's gone misty
she wants to keep him near.

She holds his hand so gently;
tears wet her wrinkled face.
She lets her mind drift back toward
another time and place.
To a time when they were young
and around them birds did sing.
To the time when their young love
flavored everything.

She yearns to have him hold her
as he used to do.
She yearns to hear him whisper
"My princess, I love you."
But that was then and in the now
not much does ease her pain.
A fleeting glance, a tiny smile,
not easy to obtain
fills her lonely heart with hope
perhaps he does remember.
His smile's a spark which warms her heart
his gift ... a fading ember.

Promotional Junkie

People know I'm not hoarder
It's not the image I portray
It's just the thank-yous I receive
From
Lancôme, Lauder, Olay.

When I go to get a lipstick
there are promos on display
"Buy some more and gifts you'll get."
Say
Lauder, Lancôme, and Olay.

So, I spend more than intended
on their phony giveaway
returning home with useless products
From
Lancôme, Lauder and Olay.

Thinking they may come in handy
if I travel far from home
I stow away these "so-called freebies"
From
Lauder, Olay and Lancôme.

Now my cupboard's nearly bursting
to my horrified dismay
with tiny packets and mini-creams
From
Lauder, Lancôme, and Olay.

Ode to Flatulence

Flatulence, oh flatulence.
How you do demean!
I was a proper lady
'till you came upon the scene
riding on the coattails of
my advancing age
another unwelcome visitor
causing me to rage!
Haven't you the decency
to at least be mute?
Is it really necessary
in company that I toot
and make other little noises
which I can't prevent,
signaling to everyone
my old anus must be spent?
The only thing that saves me
from this entire mess
are friends who by ignoring
respect my vain distress.
They pretend not to hear
the toot, the poof, the sound
as I play the innocent,
with eyes cast to the ground.

Golden Limericks

There once was an old lady from Kent
who thought her sex urges were spent.
'Till a new gent arrived,
and with her libido revived
back on to the saddle she went.

There once was a time in our past
when we thought sex in old age didn't last.
And though it's a changing
with a little arranging
we still can come off with a blast.

Migrating Follicles

A funny thing has happened
Hair seems to have changed place
Gone from where it used to grow
It now appears upon my face

Strangers

We were strangers at one time
The time before we became friends
lovers
partners
I was leery of you
you were wary of me
And then you smiled
We talked
We touched
We loved
Until life intervened
and we became strangers once again

Past Due

They had been playing nicely together
when the tiny girl started to cry
 "What's wrong, my dear?" asked Grandma.
This was the sad reply:

"I don't care what my Mummy says
I am keeping you.
I won't let her throw you out
just 'cause you're past-due."

"Who gave you that idea?"
asked Grandma in dismay.
"Mummy told me that was why
 she threw things out the other day."

She says she saw it on the box
when something's very old
it's no longer healthy
it may even have some mold.

"But I don't care what boxes say
I don't care if you have mold
I'm going to keep you anyways
even if you are old."

Lesson for an Old Soul

She sat on the sidewalk
Dog at her side
Her eyes dull and deaden
how could I abide
just walking on passed her?
But that's what I did
I ignored the poor soul
who fell off the grid
of life as we know it.
Yet what do I know
if the smallest humanity
I neglected to show
for a person whose suffering
was so plain to see
by my turning away
what does that say about me?
And the pride that I take
in being well-known
if I can't step outside
my own comfort zone.

A young boy walked over.
He patted her dog
and her face it lit up
like the sun through a fog.
True, some may question
whether a gesture so small
can make a real difference
to one in free-fall?
But that's all that it took ...
by acknowledging her there
the boy said in the moment,
"I see you. I care."
So, I thank the young boy
who taught this old soul
that a smile costs one nothing.
Now when out for a stroll
I acknowledge these people
who so often feel spurred,
and I greet them respectfully
with a smile and kind word.

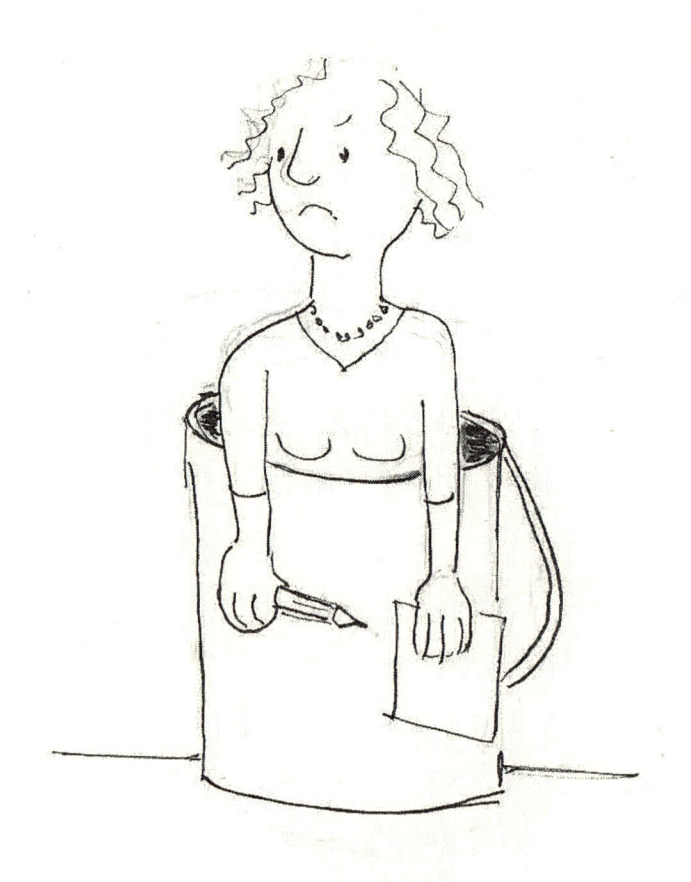

The Bucket List

Seems everyone has a bucket list,
is something wrong with me?
I wrack my brain but can't come up
with a place that I MUST see.
It's not that I have travelled much
and I wouldn't mind a cruise,
but bottom line I think it's just
a clever PR ruse
to tell old folks "Before you die
more places you must view."
That's fine for some, but others
in this golden-age milieu...
have lost the urge to fantasize
and simply put ... resist,
spending their remaining time
on a pre-death, travel list.

True, I often feel a yearning
in the middle of the night,
to do some things left undone
before the dimming of my light.
That's why I fill my bucket
with grandkids in my mind
by doing something meaningful.
Translated I'm now inclined
to break some long-time habits.
Change many of my ways,
like my careless use of plastic
and other throw-a-ways.
I attempt to make a difference,
albeit just a trace,
to leave the oceans for those to come
a less polluted space.

Google Woes

Just when I am slowing down
the world is speeding up.
Bombarding me with info
'till I think I'm on the cusp,
of dementia or some other
dreaded brain disease.
With so much to remember
how can I feel at ease?

Once upon a time ago
I thought Google was my friend.
Now when I search for something
turns out there is no end
to the ads which appear
in the middle of what I seek.
It drives me somewhat nutty.
It makes me want to shriek.

"If I want dresses, Google,
or other things you sell,
I'll do the searching by myself
Don't need you to find Chanel."

I guess I must just "suck-it-up"
as the young ones often say.
Or "get with it" I could do that
if I only knew the way
to reach someone at Google
and ask them what to do.
To tell them it isn't fair
what they put we elders through.

But calls by phone are now passé
we must converse on line.
A daunting task for those of us
whose brains are in decline

Vodka

Vodka is a friend of mine
She has virtues I enshrine
She helps me write
She helps me rhyme
but only if I treat her fine
and never, ever cross the line

Now that I am past my prime
I'm hostage to my alkaline
I must obey its bottom line
which means I no longer
do combine
my Vodka
with a glass of wine.

Not This Too!

When almost done I did think
I'd covered every base
addressing all the changes
we oldies must embrace.
But alas, alack, and woe is me
Mother Nature was not done
surprising me in subtle ways,
she sought to have more fun.

It came about so slowly
I didn't realize
that my teeth were moving.
Until...
         before my eyes,
lipstick appeared upon my teeth,
EVERY SINGLE TIME.
Something that never was
when I was in my prime.

"Buck teeth's to be expected."
My dentist said to me,
"But that can be corrected...
braces are the key."
"No way will I wear braces!"
I began to shout,
"My back, my eyes, I must repair.
Damn teeth can just stick out!"

Several Decades Later

Not since my wedding day
did I work so hard on me,
trying to erase some flaws
I feared others would see.
Lost some weight, cut my hair,
squirted Botox here and there.
Bought myself a lovely dress
blew my budget I confess
I did it for a worthy cause
simply put, it was because...

It's decades since childhood friends
I've had a chance to meet
and with the reunion looming
I admit I had cold feet.
I've been a bit successful
I can hang my hat on that...
but Carol is a doctor
and Sue-Ann a diplomat.

Sure, I know it's not a contest
to weigh what each has done,
so, I will just "suck it up"
go in and have some fun.
Oh no, that really cannot be,
my once so handsome crush
with shoulders round, head bent down
he now resembles slush!
And look at Jill, who's perky boobs
were the envy of us all
No longer is she flaunting them
now since they began to fall.

Bob and Syd, they're here too
"Dummies" who failed each test
Bragging now for all to hear
how they've surpassed the rest.
"We didn't go to college."
Their voices boom with glee.
"But we've made it to the 1%
without need of a degree."

It has been fun to see old friends
have a chance to reminisce.
However, death has taken some
who I shall truly miss.
And others haven't fared that well
I could see it in their eyes
Adversity has visited them
I only can surmise.

We all know aging takes a toll
but it's sad nevertheless.
It goes to show how dumb I was
to let my aging face cause stress.

Dirty Eyes, Really?

Coffee's On, they call it.
It's their time to sit and chat
indulging in some gossip
and a lot of 'this' or 'that.'
But one day the conversation
turned serious indeed.
Talks of films and favorite books
quickly did recede
when one of the women present,
to my utmost surprise,
asked everyone sitting there
what they do for their "dry eyes."
Since many seemed to share her fate
several suggestions did appear.
Then came a shocking comment
I never expected to hear.
"It means your eyes are dirty,"
her doctor bluntly said.
Surely, he could've coached his words
eased into it instead!
"To correct this nasty problem
on diligence I must insist.
It means three drops twice a day,
added to your to-do list."
Another thing! Who has the time?
Those lists of ours keep growing,
it's like we're trying to clear a path
while the snow's still snowing

Before that day, I never thought
that my eyes were dry
now they do feel scratchy
and I'm left to question why.
Does it mean my eyes aren't "clean"?
Do I need drops as well?
Should a doctor I go to see
this nonsense to dispel?
They're plenty things I know I have,
why expose myself to more,
knowing I'll just pick-up things
I hadn't bargained for?
Best to avoid those meetings
that put boo-boos on parade,
Since I have lost the energy
to change lemons to lemonade.

Moving Parts

My aging body I must say
is in quite a stage of disarray.
And despite the fact I disapprove
my body parts are on the move.
Behold my spine an inch it lost,
which makes me more than somewhat crossed,
'Cause if aging means we shrivel so
why does my nose continue to grow?
And my boobs, which once so proudly stood
have found a brand-new neighborhood.
They've dropped right down
and come to rest upon my stomach.
Then as you've guessed, my belly rounded
to accept these friends.
Nor is that where this all ends
'Cause gravity and extra weight
joined up to make my butt inflate.
So sadly now, I'm out of whack,
just everywhere - from front to back.
I look at me and see a mess
But I don't allow myself to stress
for what's the point of feeling sad
it's just pay-up time for years I had.
Because nothing in life is ever for free
these changes are simply my
        User-Fee.

Facing the Inevitable

My memory is slipping.
The time may come when I will no longer
recognize you, my dear friend.

And before I reach that final day.
Before disease takes my words
Before what we all fear
has become my new reality
there are things I must not leave unspoken.

I fear I may have already waited too long.
Words are harder to come by now.
But even if words do exist to adequately
express appreciation for our lifelong friendship,
I don't think I ever had them.
At least now I have an excuse.

I want to thank you for the gift of you.
For all the best parts of you, that you shared with me.
For the fun, the adventures, the times you held my hand
and for those other times
when you didn't really get where I was coming from
but you supported me nevertheless.

And now that I'm entering a place
where you cannot follow
nor would I want you to.
You mustn't fret.
It won't be so bad
and if it is I won't remember.
(That's the last of my silly jokes, I promise)

So I bid you good-bye.
I leave with my heart overflowing
with gratitude for all we've shared
for all we've meant to each other
decade after decade after decade.
And I leave with the hope that
when it appears as if all is gone
my heart will continue to beat with love,
a love that will not be relinquished
even though the brain has ceased to remember.

Thoughts for my Granddaughter

If I weren't past seventy, I'd write a rhyme
praising the virtues of passing time.
I'd skip the new wrinkles and the hair turning grey
and flippantly tell you, "It's just nature's way
of granting diversity to the roles that we play."
If I weren't past seventy.

If I weren't past seventy, I'd toast you, my friend,
with wit and with wisdom, youth's special blend,
avoiding to mention the weight you will gain,
or the sad, but true fact, that your sex life will wane.
If I weren't past seventy.

If I weren't past seventy, I'd still be in tune,
with the joys I know you'll be experiencing soon,
with the chances and challenges lying ahead,
the smorgasbord of choices in front of you, spread.
If I weren't past seventy.

If I weren't past seventy, I wouldn't know that regret
comes whenever a challenge's not met.
That living with 'what if' is much harder to do
than failing while trying to do something new.
If I weren't past seventy.

If I weren't past seventy, I mightn't realize
how quickly things change, how fast the time flies.
That small seeds planted while still in our prime
become heart-warming memories to sustain us in time.

I wouldn't have known to tell you all this...
If I weren't past seventy.

An Octogenarian's Ode to Sex

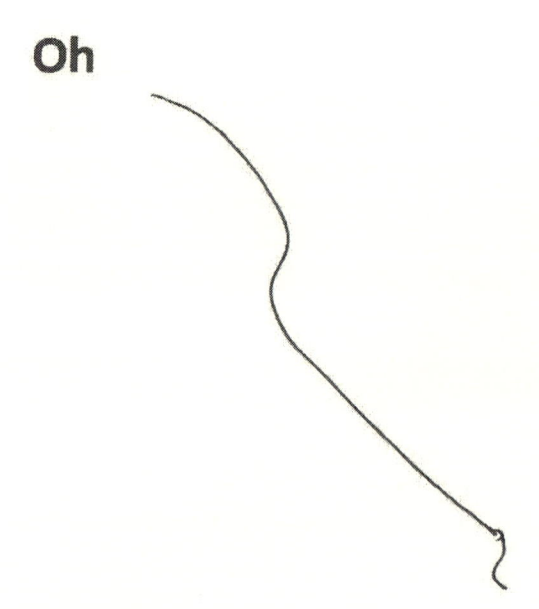

Oh

Pre-Viagra

Birthdays come and birthdays go
and each one takes its toll
Some search the mirror for ravages
while others search their soul
More oft than not, men do decide
that aging lines don't matter
Nor do they seem to care
when they've grown somewhat fatter
What is it then mature men fear
what sends their hearts a loop?
I'll tell you in all confidence –
It's called:
 The PENAL DROOP!
A plague, a curse, a pox so bad
the mighty crumble, the meek go mad.
They wear gold chains, buy fancy cars
smell up a room with choice cigars
But nothing helps this time of life
not even a young trophy wife!
For when it strikes, the guy is caught
Even oyster consumption comes to naught
The droop just droops, which is a pity
With a drooping droop, one can't feel witty,
nor fun, nor sexy, nor tantalizing
One sits and prays for the droop to start rising.
And so dear friend, while you can,
have sex with your wife or your madam,
Party with friends, run all about,
forget your sore back, overlook your damn gout.
When awaking each morning, rejoice in the rise
Never taking for granted how its grown in size.
Just stroke it gently. Use it with care
By prolonging the droop, you're prolonging despair.

The Lord Giveth, The Lord Taketh Away

"The Lord giveth, The Lord taketh."
So, goes the Bible verse
and aging is just like that,
a blessing and a curse.

It giveth years to enjoy
the wonders of our life,
but taketh away eventually
a husband or a wife.
It giveth us a freedom
to travel and to roam,
yet costly insurance fees
keep us close to home.
It giveth us the luxury
to sleep in when we want,
until our bladders wake us
for the usual bathroom jaunt.

And so ye bible doubters
it's time to realize,
The Good Book has a message
it wants to emphasize.
We can choose to complain
or to instead rejoice
in every blessed moment.
We're free to make that choice

We only need remember,
when the going, it gets tough.
To focus on the positive
and ignore the other stuff.

Which often is much easier said than done

The Girls

Once they called us "ladies"
That sat quite right with us
When "women" came into vogue
some considered that a plus.
Words will keep on changing
as life around us swirls
But as far as we're concerned
We'll forever be --"the girls."

Ode to Exercise

It's good to move the body
to make the juices flow.
It's good to stretch and bend
at least they tell me so.

And so, I put on music
to put me in the grove.
I try, I do. Let's face it
I really hate to move!

Can shopping be an exercise?
Don't say no too quick.
It can be of benefit,
depends on the parts we pick.

Shop, and arms we exercise,
muscles flex and strain,
lifting garments off the rack
returning them again.

Legs get their daily workout
as we walk from aisle to aisle
Searching for things to buy
takes many a fit-bit mile.

Put on a dress, never look
'till the tummy is pulled in.
This benefits the abdomen
keeps it toned and thin.

Balance needs be a part
of our daily exercise
Buying shoes may fit the bill
as I'll conceptualize.

Try on a shoe and lift your leg
Stand on one, then switch
Try balancing without a squirm,
(though you're allowed a twitch.)

The arms, the legs, tummy too
we neglected not a place.
'cause smiling as we shop will then
exercise muscles on our face.

Hurray for us we've done it
We've exercised – we're fit
We shopped for health and loved it
though our wallet took a hit.

On Thin Ice

The ice is thin
upon which we tread.
Each morn we wake
and think with dread,
what's nature got
in store today?
What gruesome trick
will she play
on a sciatic nerve
an arthritic joint?
We never know
and that's the point
How can we stifle
woes and fears,
and enjoy instead
these Golden Years,
without a murmur
of disease?
Tell me Doctor
Tell me, please.

My Legacy

I'm fast approaching eighty
and I think of the time to come
when death will take me away from you.
And I wonder.
Will I have a chance to say good-bye?
Will I be able to tell you one last time
how much you mean to me?
Will I show courage?
Will I even be aware?

I'm fast approaching eighty,
time to reflect upon my legacy.
Not on things amassed over a lifetime,
for, in the end, that's just "stuff"
and you never were one to value "stuff."
    And so, my precious, child
I shall leave you with my book of memories
selfishly hoping...
part of me shall remain with you,
when the rest of me is long gone.

A Life Well Spent

My life's 'bout over
I've had quite a run
had days of rain
had days of sun.
To myself
I did stay true.
Somethings worked out.
some things
I blew.
Loved my family
and friends galore
Had a life of blessings.
Can't ask for more.

Sharon Wolfe, mother of three, grandmother of six, moved to Toronto with her husband Paul in 1996, having spent all her early years in Montreal.

She's been a teacher, Human Right's Activist, Political Policy Advisor, Refugee Board Commissioner, Mediator and the Producer/Director of Abilities Festival - A Celebration of Disability Arts and Culture.

Sharon has been writing whimsical verse as far back as she can remember. Many of her ditties found their way to birthdays, anniversaries and other celebrations. However, she didn't consider publishing her endeavours until encouraged to do so while attending the Writers' Circle in Sun City, California.

Conrad the Collector, her first children's book is about a young boy, not like other boys. He doesn't like baseball or ice cream or messy rooms. Some kids think he's weird. But Conrad doesn't care. He likes what he likes and what he likes most is using his extra-special imagination to find out-of-the -ordinary "you'd never believe this" objects to add to his collections.

The Day We Planted Grammy, Sharon's second children's book follows five-year-old Cindy on an emotional journey from fear to acceptance as she comes to terms with the death of her beloved grandmother.

Sharon's books can be purchased on **Amazon.com** and **Amazon.ca.** Follow Sharon on her Facebook page: Sharon Wolfe, Author

Acknowledgements

My heartfelt thanks to Eileen Cinque who readied this book for publication. Eileen, without your patience, encouragement and publishing experience this book may never have left my computer. Your assistance proved invaluable. Thank you.

I have much love and appreciation for my brother, Saul Miller, who did the illustrations. Saul, this book means all the more to me because we worked on it together. Thank you so much.

My thanks go as well to Laara Maxwell who set aside her work to respond to my many questions. Thank you, Laara, for your wise and astute editorial comments.

Thank you to my good friend and Sun City mentor, Marc Frederic, aka Mr. Whimsy, for his ongoing encouragement and for the early edit of the poems.

I wish to mention with great love and appreciation my daughter, Lisa Wolfe, who interrupted her writing and time-consuming volunteer work to offer important insights and critiques.

To my husband, Paul, who always pays the largest price when I become obsessively involved in one project or another -- for your understanding, respect and on-going support, I am eternally grateful. I love and appreciate you beyond measure.

And finally, never to be forgotten I want to thank all my friends in Montreal, Toronto and Sun City whose tales of joys and woes have inspired so many of these poems. My love to you all.

In lieu of an index,
you may wish to record the page numbers of your
favorite verses for easy retrieval.

Made in the USA
Middletown, DE
25 February 2022